A Child's Guide
To
California
Wildflowers

Book One

Mountains & Foothills

Written & Illustrated

by

Carol Franco

Copyright 2003©Carol Franco
All rights reserved.

Published by
Mountain Lily Treasures
PO Box 3457
Idyllwild, CA 92549
(909) 659-5791

Library of Congress Number Cataloging-in-Publication Data is available.

International Standard Book Number (ISBN)

0-615-12504-0

Printed in China

First Edition, First Printing
10 9 8 7 6 5 4 3 2

Designed by Crone House Publishing & Graphics
Idyllwild, California

Photograph on Page 3 - Carol Franco

This book is dedicated to
my sweet inspirations,
Annelyse and Trevor.

THANK YOU!

Along my own journey of wildflower discovery, I've been helped by friends and family. Love and appreciation goes to Jenny, Lisa, Mary, and Mom, who encouraged and supported my dream. Mark Tilchen and Kate Kramer gave expert guidance and feedback. Anne Fratzke and Julia Youngman carefully proofread every word! The design expertise of Nancy Layton, at Crone House Publishing & Graphics, was instrumental in making this book a reality.

Thank you to one and all!

Table of Contents

Introduction

No child is too young to fall in love with wildflowers. Even small babies respond to their beauty.

It is natural for children to love wildflowers and to want to pick them. In some cases, that is quite acceptable. Most times, though, it is best to leave them so that their seeds will fall to the ground, germinate, and grow again. Birds and other wild creatures depend on many wildflowers for food and shelter. **There are many places, such as national and state parks and reserves, where picking wildflowers is strictly prohibited. Please, always check with the appropriate agencies if you are unsure of the regulations.**

This book includes a packet of wildflower seeds for a child to plant, care for, and watch grow. They can have their very own colorful flowers to pick or to leave for their feathered and furry friends.

Half the fun is in identifying the flowers and knowing a little about them. Note pages have been included in the back of the book where the child can catalog the flowers found while hiking. Hopefully, entire families will share in this delight of discovery as they explore the wonderful world where wildflowers abound!

Meet Buzzy and Merry!

Hello, Merry! Let's go find some of the wildflowers that grow in California! We'll carry pollen from blossom to blossom, too! Pollen sticks to our legs and bodies and is needed by most flowers, so we are very important!

This is going to be so much fun, Buzzy! The flowers in our book are placed in the order we might see them as we fly from the foothills to high up in the mountains. And, I'm going to sip some sweet nectar, too!

Indians used the roots as a pain killer and cooked the leaves to eat as a vegetable.

California Poppy

Color: Golden orange, red, yellow, or cream

Size: Plants are 6 in. to 2 ft. tall. Flowers are 1 in. to 2 in. wide.

Blooms: February - November

Where: Fields and foothills

Early Spanish Californians cooked the petals with olive oil. Then they rubbed the mixture on their heads to make their hair thicker. I wonder if that would work for me?

California Poppy
California State Flower - so pretty!

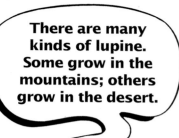

There are many kinds of lupine. Some grow in the mountains; others grow in the desert.

Coulter's Lupine

Color: Blue to lilac. Banner petals are the wide upper petals and have a yellow spot.

Size: Plants are 8 in. to 16 in. tall. Flowers are 1/2 in. wide.

Blooms: January - May

Where: Open fields and hillsides throughout Southern California

They're all pretty, but watch out for the Stinging Lupine. Its stiff, yellow bristles sting worse than you, Buzzy!

Coulter's Lupine
Grows so easily!

Clarkia

Color: Rose, pink, or lavender

Size: Plants are 1 ft. to 3 ft. tall. Flowers are 2 in. wide.

Blooms: May - August

Where: Open fields on foothills

Clarkia
Brightens dry hillsides!

This isn't really grass, but the leaves look like a kind of grass.

California Blue-Eyed Grass

Color: Blue to dark purple blossoms

Size: Plants are 4 in. to 16 in. tall. Flowers are 1 in. to 1 1/2 in. wide.

Blooms: February - July

Where: Open, grassy areas

Hey! I don't see any blue eyes, either!

California Blue-Eyed Grass
Grows from lowlands to mountains!

Indians thought the bulbs were gifts from the gods. They cooked and ate them.

Splendid Mariposa Tulip (or Lily)

Color: Usually pink, but sometimes purple blossoms can be seen.

Size: Plants are 6 in. to 2 ft. tall. Blossoms are 1 1/2 in. to 2 in. wide.

Blooms: May - June

Where: Rocky or dry open areas

Hey, Buzzy, they named this one after me! Mariposa means butterfly in Spanish!

Splendid Mariposa Tulip (or Lily)
Beautiful in any color!

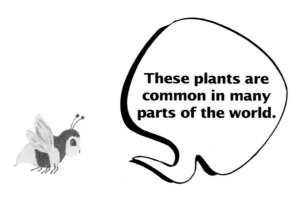

These plants are common in many parts of the world.

Fiddleneck

Color: Dark yellow to gold

Size: Plants are 6 in. to 3 ft. tall. Flowers are only 1/2 in. to 3/8 in. wide.

Blooms: March - June

Where: Mountains, foothills and flatlands where it is dry and sunny

I bet some people call them weeds!

Fiddleneck
Curls like the neck of a violin!

The bulbs can be cooked and eaten. It's better to leave the plants alone to bloom again, though.

Rosy Fairy Lantern

Color: Red

Size: Plants are 6 in. to 2 ft. tall.

Blooms: April - June

Where: Semi-shaded woods in the Sierra Nevada foothills

If the bulbs are eaten, then there won't be any lanterns for the fairies to light!

Rosy Fairy Lantern
So pretty on dry hillsides!

19

The wild iris has pretty cousins growing in many home gardens.

Wild Iris

Color: Lavender, cream, or pale yellow

Size: Plants are 2 in. to 16 in. tall. Flowers are about 3 in. wide.

Blooms: May - June

Where: Dry, wooded hillsides

I have pretty cousins, too!

Wild Iris
Look for these where big trees grow!

Miner's Lettuce

Color: Green leaves with tiny white blossom clusters

Size: Plants are 4 in. to 12 in. tall. Leaves are 2 in. to 3 in. wide.

Blooms: June - July

Where: Shady, moist places

Miner's Lettuce
Has rounded, shiny leaves!

Indian Paintbrush

Color: Red bracts are actually leaves. The flowers are white and almost hidden.

Size: Plants are 1 ft. to 3 ft. tall.

Blooms: May - September

Where: Wet meadows

Indian Paintbrush
Brightens wet meadows!

Berries can be made into jam, but birds love berries, too. I think we should save them for the birds.

Bunchberry

Color: Green leaves and white bracts with greenish blossoms

Size: Bracts are up to 4 in. tall. Bloom clusters are very small.

Blooms: June - August

Where: Moist woodlands

I sure wish I had a beak so I could eat those berries, too!

Bunchberry
A pretty sight along the road!

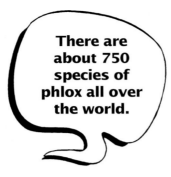

There are about 750 species of phlox all over the world.

Spreading Phlox

Color: Pink or white

Size: Plants spread 4 in. to 12 in. wide with very small flowers.

Blooms: May - August

Where: Open areas in the mountains

Let's hop on a jet so we can see them all!

Spreading Phlox
Sunshine is very important!

These flowers have some of the best pollen anywhere.

Fire Penstemon

Color: Bright red

Size: Plants are 1 ft. to 3 ft. tall. Flowers are 1 in. to 1 1/2 in. long.

Blooms: March - August

Where: Rocky or dry mountain slopes

What a great place for a B & B Inn...Butterfly & Bee Inn, that is!

Fire Penstemon
Found in surprising places!

There are many, many different kinds and colors of penstemons.

Grinnell's Penstemon

Color: Deep to pale pink

Size: Plants are 6 in. to 2 ft. tall. The largest flowers can be about 1 in.

Blooms: April - August

Where: Dry mountain slopes

I love bright pink flowers best!

Grinnell's Penstemon
Smells good!

There are other kinds of columbines in a variety of pretty colors.

Crimson Columbine

Color: Red and yellow blossoms

Size: Plants are 1 ft. to 4 ft. tall. Flowers are about 2 in. long.

Blooms: April- August

Where: Along streams and in moist woods

Watch out! Here come the hummingbirds! They love the sweet nectar of these flowers.

Crimson Columbine
Looks so delicate but is very hardy!

Young leaves can be used as herbs and to make tea. Best of all, the pollen makes the most delicious honey!

Red Fireweed

Color: Reddish purple

Size: Plants are 2 ft. to 9 ft. tall! Flowers are 2 in. long or longer!

Blooms: March - August

Where: They are one of the first plants to appear after a forest fire, but also grow well in wet areas and meadows.

I guess we don't have time for a tea party. There's too many more flowers to see!

Red Fireweed
Flowers turn to silky fluff!

Ray flowers are yellow and look like petals. Disk flowers are all the tiny little flowers in the center that look like a cone.

California Cone Flower

Color: Greenish disk flowers shaped into a cone above a ring of yellow ray flowers

Size: Plants are 2 ft. to 6 ft. tall. Flowers are about 3 in. wide.

Blooms: July - September

Where: Mountain meadows

Hey! I thought we were having ice cream - you know, cones. Ha!

California Cone Flower
Has a tall cone of tiny disk flowers in the middle!

Some people call them "Mad Violets"!

Jeffrey's Shooting Star

<u>Color:</u> Pink and yellow blossoms

<u>Size:</u> Plants are 6 in. to 2 ft. tall. Flowers are 1 in. wide.

<u>Blooms:</u> May - August

<u>Where:</u> Wet mountain meadows

They don't look mad to me. I think they're happy to be here.

Jeffrey's Shooting Star
Unusual & pretty!

I like to crawl around inside these flowers and gather pollen.

Gentian

Color: Purple or blue

Size: Plants are 2 in. to 16 in. tall
Flowers are 1 in. to 1 1/2 in. long.

Blooms: July - September

Where: Wet mountain meadows

You work too hard! It's more fun to just flutter by.

Gentian
Loves rich, wet soil!

There are many other kinds and colors of wild lilies.

Sierra Tiger Lily

Color: Yellow to red/orange with deep red or purple spots on the petals

Size: Plants can be up to 5 ft. tall. Blossoms are 2 in. to 3 in. wide.

Blooms: May - July

Where: Wet thickets in the Sierra Nevada mountains

Shhh! I want to listen to them growl!

Sierra Tiger Lily
Wild lilies are becoming rare!

The flowers have very large petals.

Subalpine Buttercup

Color: Bright yellow flowers

Size: Plants are 2 in. to 10 in. tall. Flowers are 3/4 in. to 1 1/2 in. wide.

Blooms: June - August

Where: Alpine slopes

Maybe we can hop from one petal to another, just like being on a trampoline!

Subalpine Buttercup
Sunny color in the mountains!

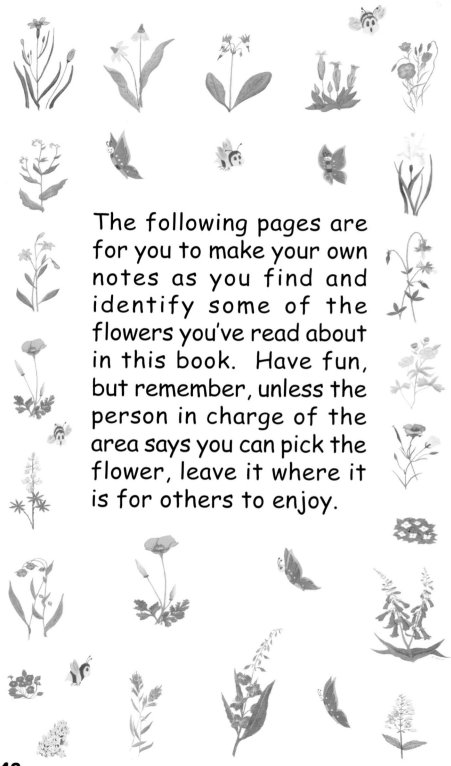

The following pages are for you to make your own notes as you find and identify some of the flowers you've read about in this book. Have fun, but remember, unless the person in charge of the area says you can pick the flower, leave it where it is for others to enjoy.

My Notes

The name of flower I found:

_____

The date and time I found this flower:

_____

The place where I found this flower:

_____

_____

What else was near this flower?

_____

_____

_____

What I liked and didn't like about this flower:

_____

_____

_____

Other notes about this flower:

_____

_____

_____

_____

_____

My own picture of this flower:

My Notes

The name of flower I found:

_____

The date and time I found this flower:

_____

The place where I found this flower:

_____

_____

What else was near this flower?

_____

_____

_____

What I liked and didn't like about this flower:

_____

_____

_____

Other notes about this flower:

_____

_____

_____

_____

_____

_____

My own picture of this flower:

My <u>Notes</u>

The name of flower I found:

_____

The date and time I found this flower:

_____

The place where I found this flower:

_____

_____

What else was near this flower?

_____

_____

_____

What I liked and didn't like about this flower:

_____

_____

_____

Other notes about this flower:

_____

_____

_____

_____

_____

_____

My own picture of this flower:

My Notes

The name of flower I found:

_____

The date and time I found this flower:

_____

The place where I found this flower:

_____

_____

What else was near this flower?

_____

_____

_____

What I liked and didn't like about this flower:

_____

_____

_____

Other notes about this flower:

_____

_____

_____

_____

_____

_____

My own picture of this flower:

My Notes

The name of flower I found:

_____

The date and time I found this flower:

_____

The place where I found this flower:

_____

_____

What else was near this flower?

_____

_____

_____

What I liked and didn't like about this flower:

_____

_____

_____

Other notes about this flower:

_____

_____

_____

_____

_____

_____

My own picture of this flower:

My Very Own Wildflower

The kind of seeds I planted:

_____

The date I planted them:

_____

The date the tiny plants appeared above ground:

_____

The date I saw the first bud:

_____

The date the first flower opened:

_____

A picture of the wildflower I planted:

Bibliography

Clarke, Charlotte B.; *Edible and Useful Plants of California*. University of California Press, Berkeley and Los Angeles. 1977

Kirk, Donald R.; *Wild Edible Plants of Western North America*. Naturegraph Publishers, Inc., Happy Camp, California. 1970

Niehaus, Theodore F., & Ripper, Charles L.; *A Field Guide to Pacific States Wildflowers*, Houghton Mifflin Co., Boston. 1976

Spellenberg, Richard; *National Audubon Society Guide to North American Wildflowers - Western Region*. Alfred A. Knopf, Inc., New York. 2001

Stocking, Stephen K., & Rockwell, Jack A.; *Wildflowers of Sequoia and Kings Canyon National Parks*. Sequoia Natural History Assn., Three Rivers, California. 1989 (Revised)

Rickett, H. W.; *Wild Flowers of America,* Crown Publishers, Inc., New York. 1953

To Order More Copies:

Simply fill out this form and send to:

Mountain Lily Treasures
PO Box 3457
Idyllwild, CA 92549

To contact us by phone, call: **(909) 659-5791**
Email: **treasures@mountainlily.com**

A Child's Guide to California Wildflowers - Book One

Please send ☐ copies to:

Name: _____   Phone: _____

Mailing Address: _____   Email: _____

City: _____ State: _____ Zipcode: _____

Price: **$10.95** each
Sales tax: Add **7.75%** for orders delivered to **California**.
Shipping via USPS, please add **$3.00 for (1) book, $2.00 for each additional book shipped to the same address.** When ordering (4) or more books, a flat rate of $2.00 per book will be charged, if all are shipped to the same address.

Enclosed is my **check** ☐ **money order** ☐
Payable to: *Mountain Lily Treasures*

Please use my **credit card**: Visa ☐   MasterCard ☐
Card number:
_____ Exp Date: _____
Name, as it appears on the card:

_____

Subtotal for book(s):	$ _____
Sales tax (CA deliveries):	$ _____
Shipping:	$ _____
Total remitted:	$ _____